Dog Friends

*Photographs of Our Best Friends,
and Their Friends*

by David J.P. Baar

website http://www.davebaar.com
e-mail   dogs@davebaar.com

© copyright 2010 by David J.P. Baar
No part of this book may be reproduced in any form, or by any electronic, mechanical, or other means, without permission from the author.

ISBN for softcover edition:
ISBN 978-0-557-75864-7

Dedication

To Dee, with whom I share life and love for these charming creatures called dogs.

*And for the dogs,
especially the Wonderful Magical GimliBear.*

Contents

Dedication • ii

Introduction • 1
    About the title • 2
    About the photography • 2

Dog Friends • 3
    Human Friends • 7

Play • 20
    Chase • 20
    Fetch • 23
    Sticks • 23
    Tug • 25
    Mock Battle • 26
    Dig • 28
    Toys • 29

Dogs At Rest • 38

Dogs In Cars • 47

Dog Portraits • 49
    Bear Portraiture • 49
    More Dog Portraits • 53
    Large Dogs • 62
        The Day of Large Dogs • 63
    Puppies • 65

Hiking and Camping • 69

Water • 73

Snow • 78

Introduction

This book is intended to be a celebration in pictures of many wonderful dogs, and their close relationships with people. Work on the book began a decade ago when my wife Dee and I first got together and began to share a series of outdoor adventures, on which I typically had a decent camera and a few lenses along. Through those adventures, we came across many charming dogs who befriended us and now appear throughout the book.

The book is organized according to themes that seem important to our shared lives with our favourite creatures, such as "play", "sticks", "fetch", and "rest", although one of the central themes for dogs, "food", is only thinly represented in this book. That absence is possibly because I tend to be more involved in providing the dog with food than in taking pictures at the time.

In the earliest years of those adventures, we began to scheme about having a four-footed creature of our own. Soon afterward, the principal character who appears often in this book, "Gimli", joined our pack as a large puppy after he found us at an animal shelter and decided we were just the couple to take him home and feed him large quantities of his favorite foods: biskies, apples, and especially, CHEESE.

The GimliBear's ancestry is a mystery but a large part of his large self is likely of Newfoundland origin, as evidenced by his sturdy build, his soft, glorious coat, his huge webbed feet, his gregarious nature, and his general inability to stay out of whatever body of water happens to be nearby. His Newf heritage is also apparent in his natural tendency to rescue large entities, particularly people and huge sticks, from the water, whether they want to be rescued or not. His prodigious drooling when in the presence of that special substance known as CHEESE, and other fine foods such as Apples and Buttered Bagels is another telltale Newfoundland sign.

The pictures span several locations across North America. The majority are from the west coast of Canada in and near Vancouver BC plus numerous camping trips on Vancouver Island and the British Columbia interior. Home for Gimli is in Vancouver near English Bay, and he often can be found swimming off Spanish Banks with the other regulars at the off-leash dog park, or accompanying us and other climbing friends in Squamish.

There also are many photos of canine characters from Ontario, New York, Oregon, and California.

About the title

The title of this book, Dog Friends, has a three-fold meaning. The book title refers to the friendships that people have with dogs, to exemplary dog friendships and play relationships with other dogs (and other creatures, real and imaginary), and to bonds between people that have come about through their shared love of dogs.

About the photography

Although a few of the photos are older, most of the photos were taken from 2001 to 2010. A wide variety of camera equipment, mostly but not entirely digital, was used. The most commonly used equipment was one of several Canon DSLR's (5D Mark II, 5D, 20D, others) and a variety of high quality EOS lenses, plus a few specialized manual lenses with EOS adapters. Some of the older photos were taken with Olympus OM series film gear. Almost all the photos were taken with "existing light", with backfill and bounce flash gear used only in a few cases, and never directly aimed at the dog. Tripods were rarely if ever used, and anyone who has tried to walk attached to a large willfull dog and take pictures at the same time will appreciate why. None of the photos were "posed" or really were pre-planned in any way, except for perhaps one notable exception in the "Camping and Hiking" section.

This book does not attempt to cover working dogs such as assistance dogs or emergency service dogs. I'll leave documenting those wonderful dogs to other authors.

This is a book of few words. From here forward, I'll mainly let the pictures speak for the dogs.

Dog Friends

This book begins now with its namesake chapter. Herein are some of my favourite pictures of dogs, in some cases with their human friends, and in others, with other dogs.

Other than that central theme of friendships, this first set of pictures is only minimally organized and ordered. I think that is appropriate since some of these canine characters seem to revel in the chaos that they create, and playing with dogs also can be a relief from our over-organized modern lives. It's only fitting to start this chapter with a picture of that canine master of chaos himself, the GimliBear, creating havoc in our kitchen.

Gimli understands that the kitchen table is an excellent place to forage for food, although one's staff seem to react rather strangely to one's presence there.

Dogs are known to form friendships with other animals. Gimli had a cat playmate as a puppy, and he occasionally makes "play bow" gestures to the neighbourhood cats, generally with little success in engagement. He even once tried to make friends with a skunk (with disastrous results). We'll stick to dogs herein.

Gimli is one of the many regulars at the Spanish Banks off-leash dog area in Vancouver, and this tour of dog friends now takes to the water there.

Fetching teamwork

Our intrepid threesome, outbound

and the successful fetch.

Duke and Gimli at Spanish Banks. Duke is a little surprised by what Gimli is carrying - a coconut!

The young Darwin and the young Winston

Zoe and Gimli, Spanish Banks regulars and pals

Human Friends

This section is in tribute to the extraordinary friendships between humans and dogs.

I've encountered some wonderful "dog people" over the years of taking the photos that appear in this book. A couple of them, Mike, "the dogfather" and Donald, "friend of many malamutes", stand out in their kindness and empathy for dogs, and in their abilities to "speak dog". The next few photos show these characters with some of their canine friends.

Mike with Caesar, and two other friends.

Sadly, dear old Caesar passed away not long after the above photo was taken. He was a fine, gentle giant of a dog, and we miss him at the Spanish Banks dog park. A friend recently remarked how dogs have such tragically short lives. We treasure the time that we spend with any of them.

Mike with dear old Ceasar. Friend Maggie is in the background.

Close friends.

Lupa with dog wizard Donald

Gimli, Dee, the late Tundra, and Donald, in the schoolyard

Joe and Margaret, circa 1980

Joe was one of two charming spaniels in my family in my formative years. This picture of Joe in my sister Margaret's arms is also illustrative of a Baar family trait, that being an innate tendency to spoil dogs. Margaret is now a veterenarian, having planned on becoming one since childhood. Joe surely helped that career choice.

Stewart and Dagney, circa 1986

Although by photographic standards, this is perhaps the poorest quality photo in this book, it is one of the most important. Dagney was a special and especially smart dog. Her close relationship with her human Stewart was remarkable, and was part of the inspiration for this book. She followed Stewart everywhere, even onto his windsurfer (after a lot of encouragement) and waited for him outside work in the Queen's University Dept. of Physics every day, yet she understood that when Stewart was away traveling, I was to be her surrogate human and she was to stay with me until he returned. Those of us fortunate to have met her will never forget Dagney.

A trio of smiling friends

The Kiss

Typical scene at the dog beach...

in typical Vancouver weather

Dee and Gimli dressed for the Vancouver rain.

Sharing a bench in Lynn Valley

Shake-a-paw after the session

High-Five

Gimli teaches "Sit" to some young friends.

It's fun to have a friendly bear in the yard.

Deb and 3 friends at "Club Fed"

"The Brats" taking their humans for a ski. Chain Lake, BC

Gimli does a fine sit at school.

Happiness is spending time with a dog.

Play

Play is central to the lives of most dogs. It has been suggested that dogs have evolved from wolves but never fully mature psychologically out of a juvenile wolf state, such that they remain playful all their lives. (Notably, a similar lack of maturity can be found in many humans, especially those with an entrepreneurial bent, and the author of this book doesn't represent an exception to that description.) Specific games and related activities are particularly common, such as Chase, Fetch, Tug, and Dig.

Chase

Chase is a simple, natural form of dog play. Watching 2 or more dogs in chase, leaping over whatever obstacles are in the way, is one of the best ways to see the grace and speed of dogs. Chase is a favourite game for Gimli, and he shows interesting behaviours within it. He's an astonishingly fast sprinter for such a burly dog, and has kept up with greyhounds at speed (yet with better cornering ability) but he'll slow down and obviously adjust his gait to match that of another dog. This seems as if intended, to let slower dogs participate. Toys may or may not be involved in chase as they are in the picture below, but we'll get into the important details of toys later.

Aussie Shepherds Henry and Angel in hot pursuit of Gimli

Evening chase, Long Beach, Tofino, BC

Fast friends in English Bay, Vancouver, BC

Gimli as the Chaser

and as the Chasee (Brohm Lake, Squamish, BC)

Fetch

Most aspects of the game of Fetch are instinctive to many dogs, although getting the dog to let go of the item that was fetched can require some training, or bribery.

a fine Fetch in progress

Sticks

Sticks deserve special mention alongside Fetch, particularly when you have a dog with a propensity to fetch the largest stick on the beach.

"Log" might be a better description.

Think of the jaw and neck forces required for this feat.

The human fetching staff should be ready for any weather (Comox, BC).

Tug

Unlike the human "tug-of-war" game, possession, rather than position, is the goal of the dog "tug" game.

On the beach, you can really dig your paws in.

Hybrid Fetch and Tug, perhaps.

Mock Battle

One of the most common forms of play between dogs is a mock battle in which the participants grapple with each other with open jaws. We've come to call this form of play "dogzilla". Often it follows a vigorous session of high speed chase. Much like the Greco-Roman wrestling that the humans do, *dogzilla* usually concludes with both participants on the ground. *Dog-*

A classic stand-up start to the Dogzilla match

zilla can appear to be quite ferocious, but rarely escalates beyond play and usually results in no harm to the participants. Normally the two-footed referees don't have to step in; the game usually finishes with one participant in a submissive position. Typically, at that point, the duelling parties separate and a new chase begins.

Dogzilla, the ground game

Dig

Dig is a varied activity. Sometimes there is a goal, such as creating a place to hide a bone or a toy, or uncovering edible treasures, but often "dig" is a game in itself.

A dual mining operation.

Heading underground with the treasure.

Toys

A depiction of dog play is not complete without a look at some important toys. A good toy collection includes the basics, such as a well-seasoned tennis ball (or several of them, spanning varying degrees of wear and sliminess), and simple is best...

Rory with her basic tennis ball

*Popular throwing tools are **sometimes** helpful.*

Balls come in a variety of sizes, sometimes to suit the dog...

The descriminating collector should have a variety of types and styles of toys to choose from ...

Squeaky toys are particularly good for getting attention of silly humans, and the louder the squeak, the better.

Imminent "Squeak"!

A complete toy collection should also have representation from several species of soft toys....

Frog

Tiger

GO-RIL-LA

Can you spot the dog (Cody) among the toys?

Water dogs need water toys...

The classic Kong

The spectacular Double Bumper Whumper

Abstract Play

Almost regardless of the chosen toy, the same silliness can ensue:

the upside-down, very much at home GimliBear in his yard

Dogs At Rest

For a dog, there's a time and a place for snoozing. The time comes often, and the place is wherever you happen to be. That can range from a comfy bed shared with a friend,

Dora and Turbo in Castlegar

to the nearest bathtub....

Gimli at maximum goofiness

Often one's humans' beds make the best sleeping places

"Do they know I'm here yet?" Rory very much at home

especially when the humans aren't around and you can take the whole bed....

A very comfortable little Bear

It's great to snooze with soft friends.

One of our couches seems to naturally become a place to sleep for many friends' dogs that we've taken care of over the years. Here, Barley is testing out the soft cushions during a brief stay with us. Later, Gimli decided to make some custom alterations to this same couch; it seemed to him to be a good place to bury a bone, and he dug through all of the cover material and stuffing to the springs in order to do that. We then had to re-cover the couch with a sturdy canvas material to make it somewhat more resistant to Gimli's destruction capabilities (see also the Sticks and Dig sections of this book for more about that). You can see the difference in the couch covering between this 2003 photo and the following images taken later, after Gimli's deconstruction efforts.

Friend Barley recovering on our couch after a hike

Time to put my big feet up for a rest with my humans

That Biology paper was enough to put me to sleep.

On adventures, you just have to make the best of what's available

The proper use of a bouldering pad

even when you can't be on level ground

Gimli at the climbing crag in Lynn Valley

The best adventures are best followed by a good snooze (overleaf)...

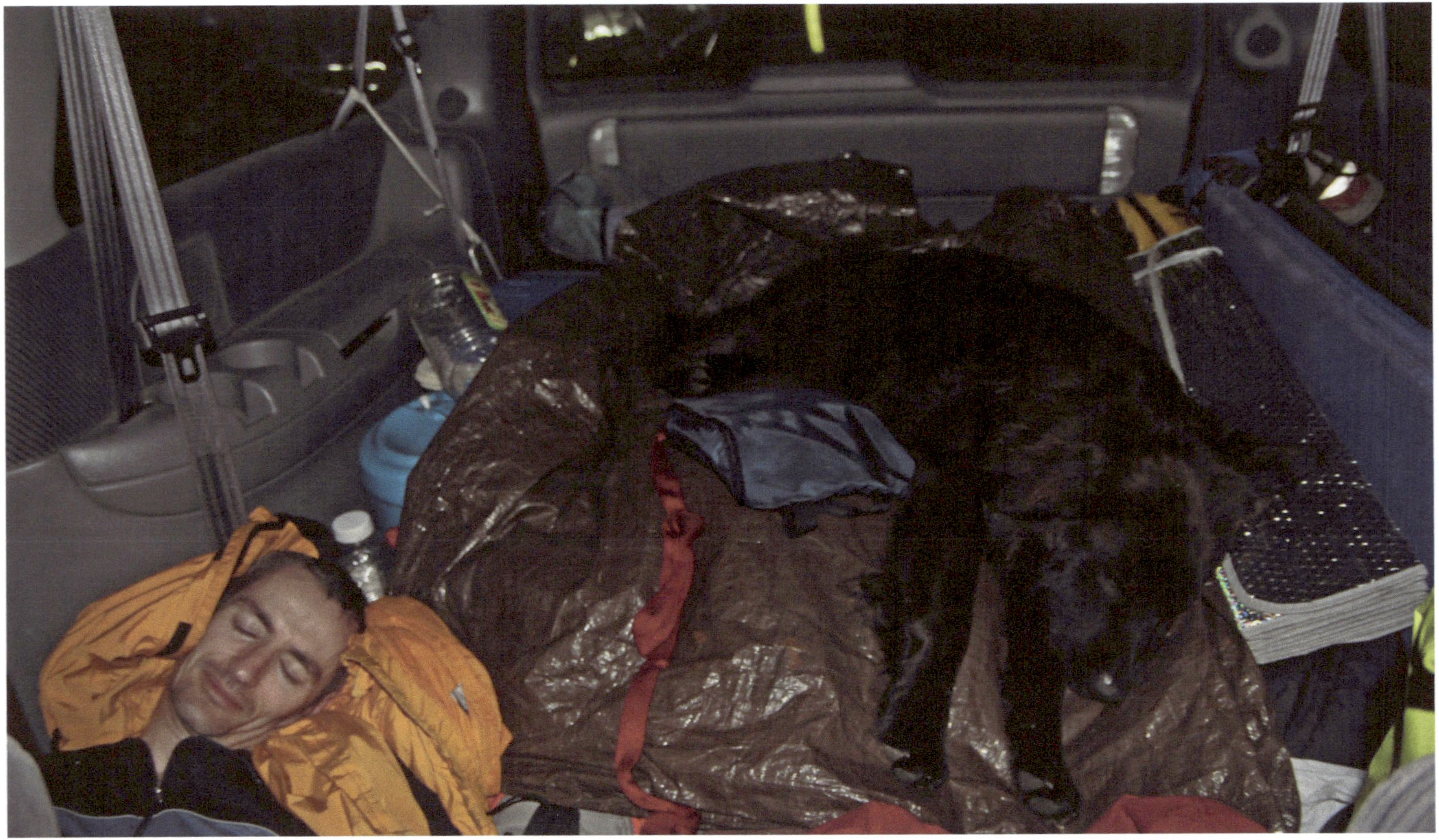

A tired GimliBear gets the best spot in the van after a long camping trip on Vancouver Island.

Still, it's great to come home to your own bed,

Gimli's special "For me?" cushion

or even a friend's bed...

A visiting friend, Zoe, on Gimli's bed

Dogs In Cars

Often the best part of an adventure is in getting there. However, it's good to know that the vehicles in all the pictures in this set were not moving.

I'm Vinnie, your driver, and I'll be taking you to Lynn Valley today.

Definitely sound asleep at the wheel

Who's watching the road?

Are we there yet?

Dog Portraits

My favourite biologist, Dee, tells me that there is a hypothesis that dogs' facial expressions have essentially evolved to be understandable by humans, and to elicit desired reactions from us. This chapter is an attempt to capture some of those expressions, but also just to present some favourite portrait-style images of some four-footed friends.

Bear Portraiture

From the first day we met dear Gimli, he exhibited an apparent philosophical side. He will often sit quietly looking out on the world, as if thinking deep thoughts and perhaps contemplating the mysteries of the universe (or else planning how to convince his humans to give him more cheese, a subject of similar importance). The staff at the SPCA shelter that we adopted him from as a puppy had actually nicknamed him "Phil", short for "philosopher", from having seen this behaviour in even the young Gimli. The photo below, which also graces the cover of this book, is to me the quintessential portrait of Gimli in his "philosophical" state. The photo was actually taken with a decent portrait lens, the stellar Canon EOS 100mm f2.

Gimli the Philosopher

However, the contrast across the states of Gimli is impressive. Compare the apparent reflective state shown above with the following photo. They are really of the same little Bear!

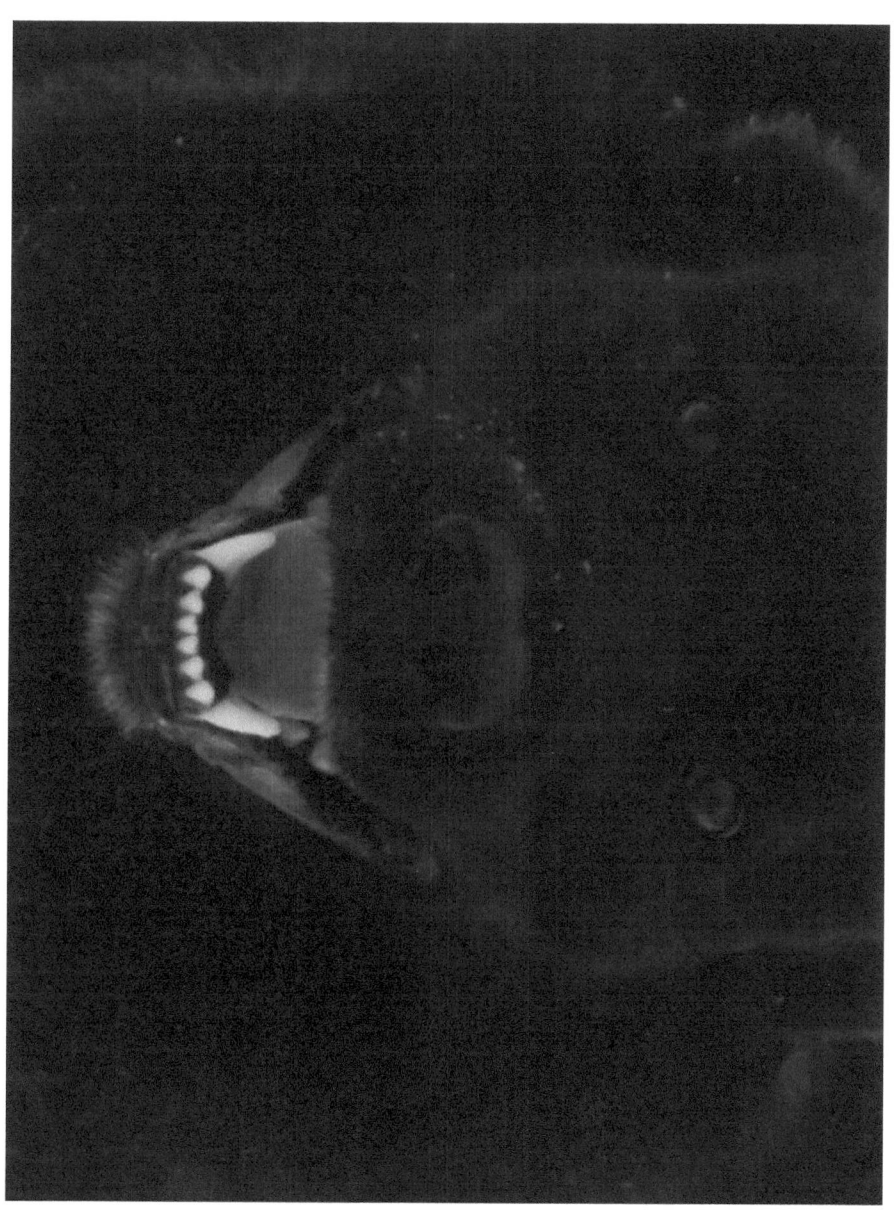

The furry Beast within

Now that you've seen the beast, some more characteristic and charming states of Gimli follow.

Gimli in snow

Gimli in his yard

Guarding the perimeter

Dog's noses are many times more sensitive than our own. I imagine that a dog experiences an especially appealing scent much as humans take in a scenic vista. Dee and I call the dog's experience a "snifta"

Gimli taking in a "snifta" in his yard

More Dog Portraits

Many of the following portraits are of dogs that have walked with us. Some of these dogs have special stories. All are simply beautiful creatures.

Gimli's friend and neighbour Zoe on the trail

Yuzu, who shared Gimli's yard for a while.

Our guide "Yellow Dog", who befriended us at Nitinat Lake, BC

"White Dog", another fine furry friend at Nitinat Lake, BC

Beautiful Airedale

The late, great Kuma

Kuma was a huge Malamute and a dear friend. He took Dee and I for walks when we first got together. Sadly, Kuma passed away a few years ago due to bone cancer.

Sarge
A 16 year-old Bassett Hound,
on Topsail Island at Bellevue Park, Sault Ste. Marie, Ontario

Rory in profile

Harper in his doggy life vest as usual, ready for a swim.

Harper is 16 years old as of this 2009 picture. He's a frequent visitor and swimmer at Brohm Lake near Squamish, British Columbia.

Baxter, an enormous Landseer Newfoundland. Baxter is big enough to deserve a whole page.

Lupa

Beautiful spotted dog at the crags, Squamish, BC

A fine Malamute at home in the snow, Squamish, BC

"The Brats", Daisy and Sadie, at The Cabin, Chain Lake, British Columbia

Large Dogs

Nothing against small dogs, but certain large dogs just seem to have a special charm to them. Their overall goofiness seems to be amplified by their size.

Maya the mastiff, holding court at Nitinat Lake, BC

"WROOOO"

A fine singing welcome from dear (and very large) Kuma

The Day of Large Dogs

One day while hiking around Buntzen Lake, BC, we encountered an extraordinary number of big dogs. The day became known as "The Day of Large Dogs". The following 2 photos are of the largest of the large.

Two sturdy mastiffs and their sturdy human relaxing at Buntzen Lake, BC. There's a bit of "dog-human convergence" going on here...

Most people think Gimli is a large dog. At >30Kg, he is. But Baxter was truly enormous, even for a Newfoundland.

Baxter and Gimli, Buntzen Lake, BC

Puppies

The charm of puppies hardly needs introduction. Here are some pictures of some beautiful four-footed friends, in their formative years.

You can put me down any time.

A young Henry with neighbour Greg and Dee. Henry later became known for more than his long ears, thanks to his mulberry tree trimming abilities.

young Vinnie

Several years ago, a particularly gregarious and affectionate Bernese Mountain Dog puppy joined our neighbourhood dog contingent. "Vinnie" developed the habit of wandering uninvited into open doors of both houses and cars in the neighbourhood. He was charming enough and so obviously friendly that he could pull this off without causing too much concern amongst the visitees. As Vinny's visiting exploits grew, and as Vinny took us for walks on adjacent blocks, we heard more and more exclamations of "I know that dog!" and "He's been to our house." The visit legends, and the dog, grew. (A more fully grown Vinnie also appears in the Dogs In Cars section of this book.)

"He's been to our house!"

Vinnie enjoying his own garden

Some dogs dislike baths, but Gimli relishes the warm water and attention.

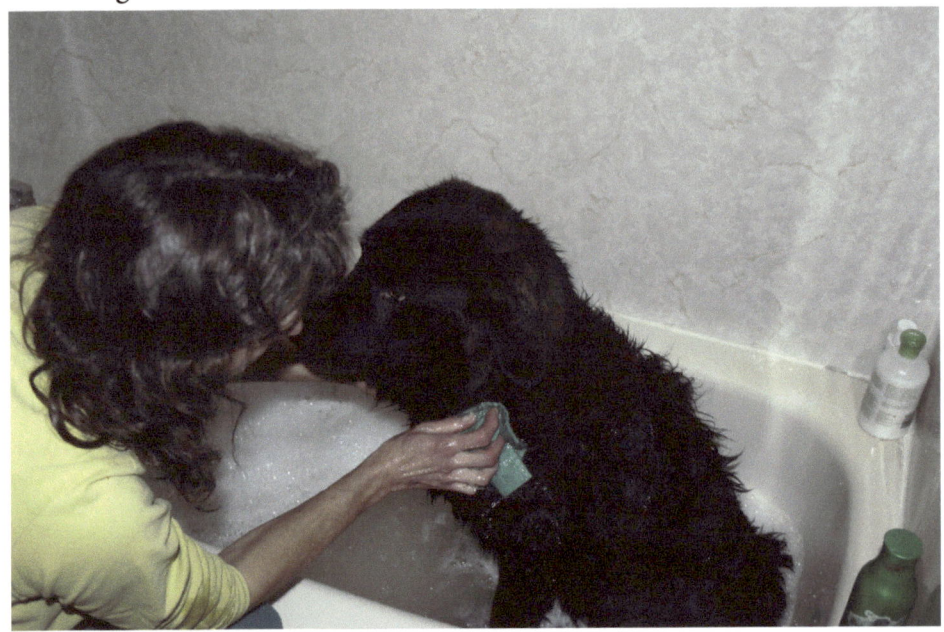

A young Gimli having one of his first baths in his home spa.

The huge head and paws were telltale signs that this little Bear wouldn't remain little for long.

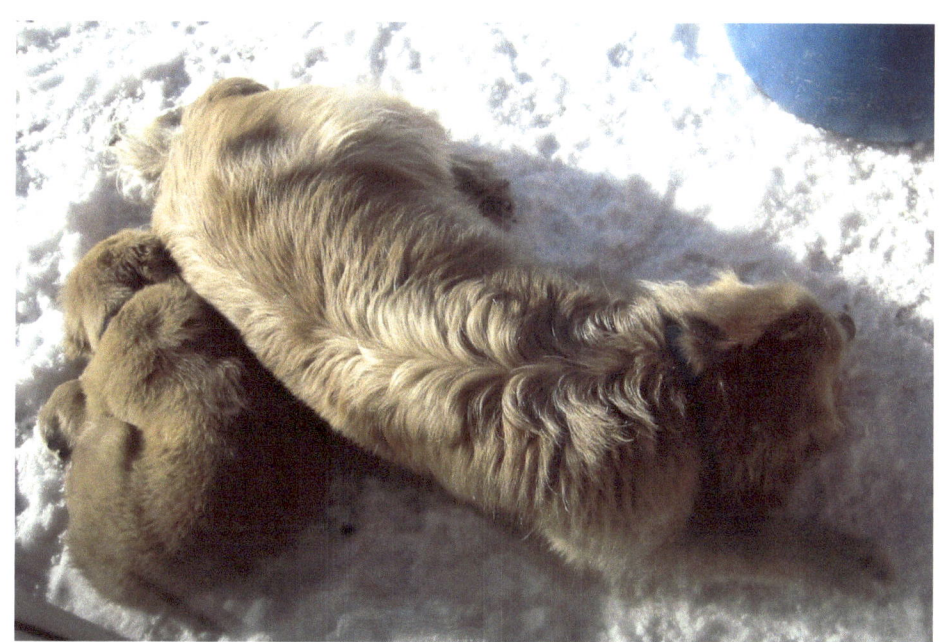

Retriever puppy and mother keeping warm in the snow

Kuma the Malamute was huge even as a puppy, clearing 100 pounds long before reaching full size. A small child meeting the much larger young Kuma for the first time exclaimed,

*"That's a **Puppy**?!?"*

Hiking and Camping

Dogs particularly enjoy hiking and camping for the outdoor adventure and fine forest smells, the companionship, and last but not least also because they present excellent close-at-paw opportunities for obtaining food, especially at the campsite.

On one of our early camping trips to Nitinat Lake, BC, before we had a dog of our own, we were befriended by a particularly gregarious dog. "Yellow Dog" began the friendship by leading us on a grand early morning tour of the forest trails, and then joined us for breakfast and relaxation afterward.

How about some of that French Toast for a hungry tummy?

We later saw Yellow Dog sprawled across his human's lap getting a relaxing tummy rub after his adventures of the day.

That was good. A very relaxed Yellow Dog

Hiking is all about stopping for lunch.

The following image might be the only picture in the book that is "staged"; Dee is holding a biscuit in front of the sign to get Gimli's interest. Gimli bears a remarkable resemblance to a bear, so we just couldn't resist.

I resemble that remark.

Are you ready yet?

One of our frequent adventure areas is Strathcona Park on Vancouver Island. We often camp near Buttle Lake there. There is a meadow at the end of the lake that Gimli loves, and that we have come to call *Gimli's Meadow*. This is one of our favourite pictures of Gimli there.

Gimli reflecting on Buttle Lake.

Water

The words "water" and "dog" are very often found together. Here are some water dogs and friends, on and in the water. Other water dog pictures appear in the "Fetch" section of this book.

A fine way to spend a warm summer day

Someone needs to move up front

Best friends enjoying a swim in Brohm Lake

Four-footed fishing guide

Gimli in flight just after high speed taxiing through shallow water off Spanish Banks

Gimli and Dee on Buttle Lake on the return from the beautiful Marble Meadows hike. Strathcona Park, BC

After a good session in the water, there's only one thing left to do...

Shake!

Snow

We are fortunate to have shared many adventures in snow with some fine four-footed companions. The pure joy that they exhibit at just being able to run freely and play in fresh snow and fresh clean air is inspiring.

Kuma and Dee at play in the UBC Endowment Lands, Vancouver, BC

Gimli flying over snow. Maximum speed and maximum joy.

Rory in fine catching form on a winter day in Kanata, Ontario

An excellent trail for those with snowshoes or very large paws

A very happy Gimli

Gimli has a strong resemblance to a bear, and has been mistaken for one many times. It's easy to appreciate why when you experience this creature hurtling towards you at high speed on a snowy trail.

Dog or bear?

It's the GimliBear.

We'll leave you with this favourite. Until our next hike together, farewell.

Dee and Gimli, Cypress Mountain, BC

WOOF. It's time for biskies…

The End.